What We Have in Common

A Brim Coloring Book

Written by Jane Landey
Edited by David Austin
Drawings by David Austin and Jane Austin

Introduction

What We Have in Common Brim Coloring Books enable children to color the drawings as they read along! The books display the similarities of related animals. In this series, the turkey and the vulture are compared.

The facts enable children to appreciate common values. Thus, imbibing in them interest towards animals which could help them appreciate what they have in common with one another.

THE TURKEY

AND

THE VULTURE

The turkey and the vulture have things in common. They are birds and they have bald heads.

The turkey and the vulture meet by the hills.

Hello Mister Vulture.

Hello Mister Turkey.

Hello! How are you this morning?

Fine! And you?

I look good!

Hey, you have no hat on.

Yes, it is not sunny today.

I carry my hat under my wing!!

You better take it off!

Why?

It does not make us look alike.

Ah! You mean my bald head and yours.
I will remove the hat now.

Yes! That's better.

I must look different today.

You have a necklace around your neck.

It is a birthday gift. Ha, Ha.

Who could that be from?

It is from my friend, Ibis.

Yea, with its bald head that makes three of us.

Anyway, two for friends, three is a crowd!

My day is always busy.

Mine too!

What do you do?

I fly round the hills!

Doing what?

Searching for food!

What kind of food?

A body that does not move!

I look for ants and insects that fly by.

Do you enjoy your meal?

Yes, I do!

I do too!

What We Have in Common Brim Coloring Books
Crocodile and Alligator
Turtle and Tortoise
Starfish and Octopus
Worm and Snake
Turkey and Vulture
Ostrich and Emu
Weka and Kiwi
Bat and Rat
Camel and Llama
Duck and Pelican
Kangaroo and Wallaby
Pig and Tapir
Skunk and Squirrel
Hedge and Anteater
Cat and Owl
Elephant and Rhinoceros
Dog and Fox
Buffalo and Bull
Leopard and Cheetah
Horse and Zebra